Class ACT

Text by John DeMers
Photographs by Michael Palumbo

Special Thanks to Our
Talented Staff of Chefs

*The New Orleans
School of Cooking*

To order our own and other Louisiana products:

(800) 237-4841
(504) 525-2665

www.nosoc.com

Introduction

Over the past two decades, the profound traditions of Creole and Cajun cuisine have attracted the attention of numberless food writers, not to mention the curiosity, admiration and, in some cases, commitment of some of this country's finest chefs. The result of this fascination - hyper-excited imports mixing with locals of talent - is a "new-style" Creole and Cajun that often has much to recommend it. Surely a cuisine born of contributions from several centuries of immigration should feel right at home with change, with evolution. But here at the New Orleans School of Cooking, generally speaking, this "new-style" cuisine is not our style.

Day after day, night after night, we face visitors and locals eager to experience what we, and most culinary historians, believe to be America's only native cuisine. In many great cities, they say, it's possible to get a terrific meal. In many great cities, it's possible to taste dishes from all over the world. But only in New Orleans, the logic goes, is it possible to settle into a meal actually born within a mile or two of the table you are occupying - sometimes, within a block or two.

That's what makes New Orleans cooking so unique. That's what makes it the fascination of chef after chef. And that's what makes it indisputably important, to every single American, everywhere.

We take our responsibility seriously, as teachers and as food evangelists. Yet as our message includes so much joie de vivre, we also try hard never to take ourselves too seriously. Food, after all, as the old Creoles and Cajun understood, is still only food. Where it finds its meaning is as part of a celebration, whether of birth (a life to be lived) or of death (a life that was lived). Or of anything in between. It's not for nothing we wear our philosophy on our sleeves, ready to explain to anyone who thinks we are a brainless party town. It didn't take us 300 years of living in New Orleans to figure out how to be brainless. It took us 300 years to figure out how to be happy.

One thing we're not when it comes to this happiness is possessive. Even though we understand vital city services would be strained past the breaking point if everybody in America suddenly decided to move to New Orleans, we are satisfied that everyone is or ought to be considering it. For ourselves, we have a long tradition of going away for money but returning for love - even when love costs us money, which of course it usually does. And we love few things better than imparting (and even exporting) our own brand of joy to places that have never seen the like. There's hardly a city in America that doesn't boast small pockets of nostalgic New Orleanians conducting Mardi Gras festivities in the days before Lent. In Fat Tuesday Anywhere USA, the banks and post office may be open, but all good New Orleanians are drinking a beer and spending hours on the telephone home.

We are, then, an unusual bunch - always have been and, with any luck, always will be - with an unusual story to tell. We tell it often and with passion in words, helped along by the hundreds of writers who've visited for a weekend and spent the rest of their careers scamming assignments that would keep them here. We tell our story in music and dance, a sensible story now that we've stopped searching for its (and our) roots in France or Spain and found it equally, whatever the color of our skin, in the African experience. And most of all, we tell it in our food. There is no writer's notebook, no painter's canvas, no jazzman's instrument that lets us tell our story quite like staring into an empty pot and knowing we need to make dinner.

In those moments, staring into that pot, we see our ancestors staring back. And in our best, if rare, moments of enlightenment, we see our children too. If we do our jobs right, if we *be* New Orleanians right, they will see, they will know, and they will understand. It would make us very happy if you, with a nudge or two from this book, begin to see, know and understand too.

An Appetizer Portion Of History

1 f you've been in New Orleans more than a couple days, or if you've been lucky enough to take one of our classes (hey, we love what we do!), you've probably heard New Orleans described as a gumbo pot. There's any number of reasons we love to say this, starting with the fact that we really love gumbo. Happily, we now introduce it to novices by explaining its roots in a West African word for okra, a word brought here by slaves who probably brought the first okra as well. This makes a lot more sense than the generations who claimed gumbo was simply our spin on French bouillabaisse. We've eaten bouillabaisse in New York and Los Angeles, Paris and even its hometown of Marseilles - and, as we like to put it here in New Orleans, bouillabaisse ain't nothin' like gumbo.

The second reason we tell you our city is a gumbo pot is because, well, it is. And after the stories you may have heard about this building or that street or that corner - you know, the ones about Marie Laveau, Jean Lafitte and Napoleon in some menage a trois aboard a pirate ship docked at the foot of Canal Street - we figure you have a healthy dose of truth coming. Our cuisine is one big well-seasoned cast-iron pot, into which generations have poured the single ingredient that mattered most: themselves. That's why so many of us see so many familiar faces when we gaze inside.

As a culture, we're slowly coming to understand better that New Orleans may feel like an Old World city, especially if you're from someplace founded in 1927. But as a culture, ours is dramatically a New World event,

the result of what happens not in some homogenized ancient setting but in some new, uncertain place where conflicting dreams battle for survival. In this battle, some lived and some died. But the smart learned to give and take. Slowly, marriage to marriage, bloodline to bloodline, a new people with a new culture was born. The French of that day borrowed a word from the Spanish for what was happening here, and criollo became Creole. They also began the conversational process by which the French-speaking country people driven here from Nova Scotia (Acadia) became known first as les Acadiens and finally Cajuns.

Recorded history tells us that New Orleans was French, then briefly Spanish, then French again even more briefly. Napoleon wanted to keep New Orleans (and a massive piece of real estate stretching to Canada) just long enough to sell it to the stupid Americans. And the Americans, led by President Thomas Jefferson, were stupid enough to want it. With the Louisiana Purchase, young America nearly doubled in size.

It must have more than doubled in complexity. French, Spanish, African and Native American, who'd had enough trouble keeping each other in line, suddenly had to deal with the lowest class of party-crasher yet - the American. And within a few decades, they had to open their weary arms again, to wave after wave of Sicilians, Irish, Germans, Greeks, Croatians and more, all apparently taking the Statue of Liberty at face value. As a city, we didn't exactly jump up from our easy chairs and hug each new dirty-faced recruit, but we did make a bit of room on the couch. The languages were many, the barroom brawls nonstop; but before long everybody married everybody else's sister and decided that getting along increased the chances of getting Sunday dinner.

It's a different world now, of course. The irony is that only now do politicians speak of diversity - we've had nothing but diversity for centuries. Only now do chefs speak of fusion - and we've had nothing but fusion as long as we've been cooking. New Orleans, so often portrayed as a city giant steps behind, is in some ways giant steps ahead. Grim survivors that we've had to be, battered by weather, famine, flood and disease, we've understood from the start the simplest, most elusive truth: We need each other.

So the next time you cook gumbo, especially if you cook it from this book, remember that we're not only all in the same boat but in the same pot as well.

A Note On the Recipes

Every recipe in this book is one we cook here in New Orleans to feed our families, to share with our friends, to impress our bosses or our spouses-to-be. Many of these recipes are dishes we prepare and teach others to prepare at The New Orleans School of Cooking. Those are the recipes we mark with a star in the index, just to let you know these are foods you're likely to find at our school in the French Quarter just about every day of life.

Here are a few more tidbits and ingredients that might help you get started cooking New Orleans cuisine our way.

ROUX: Used to be, young Creole and Cajun cooks were introduced to their art form with the words "First you make a roux." Increasingly, though, this thickening and flavoring mix of oil and flour is used sparingly at the end of the cooking process, affording the cook a greater degree of control. Louisiana's chefs could write volumes on making a roux, from the lightest to the darkest, always without burning the mix as it's stirred. Let's hope fear of fat never makes the making of terrific roux a dying art.

TRINITY: You might think we're talking about religion all the time, but when Louisiana cooks mention the Trinity, they mean the mixture of three seasoning vegetables that form the basis of just about every Creole or Cajun savory dish. The three? Onion, green pepper and celery, of course. These are usually sauteed in somewhere between a little and a lot of fat, depending on how much the cook is watching his or her waistline. They turn transparent and just the slightest bit sweetly caramelized. They'll be perfect.

STOCK, BROTH, ETC.: Used not just in soups but in the many varieties of stews we love in south Louisiana, stock offers the home cook a handful of choices. The best thing to do is make stock, naturally. Take the bones of chicken, beef, duck, turkey, seafood or just a mixture of vegetables and simmer them in water until an intense stock forms. It's super-easy, but it does take time. If you prefer,

you can substitute canned broth or bouillon made from dried powder or cubes. Traditionally, intense dried stocks known as "bases"were sold only to restaurants, but they are now entering the home cooking market as well.

ANDOUILLE: Called by the same name it often carries in France, this is south Louisiana's smoked sausage extraordinaire. Traditionally, it's made of pork - a byproduct of the festive autumn or winter boucherie. Today, of course, only a handful of residents make their own. The taste tends to be peppery, but the smoked flavor is more important to most recipes than any amount of spice.

JOE'S STUFF: Here's a shortcut home cooks can learn from professional chefs: mix your seasonings in advance. Better still, find a mix you really love and buy it. Here at the New Orleans School of Cooking we mix, use (and really love) our own seasoning blend, Joe's Stuff, which is cited in several of our recipes. There are plenty of other Creole and Cajun mixes available; feel free to substitute your personal favorite.

HOT SAUCE: For Louisiana food fetishists seeking a shortcut to searing flavor, a number of old families have just the thing. All these entrepreneurs take some version of Tabasco, jalapeno or habanero peppers, reduce them to a fiery mash, then extend them into a sauce with vinegar and other liquids. Louisiana hot sauces are sold in almost every country on earth.

FILE: Pronounced more or less like fillet and filet, this is a powder made by grinding dried sassafras leaves. It's an old Choctaw trick, picked up by the European settlers around New Orleans and still used as a thickener in gumbo. You'll see "file gumbo" on some menus around town, which almost certainly means no okra was used to thicken during cooking. And you'll hear of it in Hank Williams' famous refrain "Jambalaya, crawfish pie... file gumbo!"

TASSO: A Cajun country pork product that's almost never eaten on its own but used as a seasoning meat. It lends its smokiness and saltiness to beans and soups - even, these days, to crawfish dishes and sophisticated cream sauces for pastas.

Appetizers

Crawfish Bread

1 pound crawfish tails
1/2 cup bread crumbs
2 Tbsp butter
1 cup Monterey Jack or
  Mozzarella cheese
1 cup onion
1/2 cup celery
1 10 oz. loaf of french bread
1/2 cup green onion
1/4 cup Joe's Stuff seasoning

Sauté onions and celery in butter, add in crawfish tails along with seasoning and cook for 3 - 4 minutes. Stir in bread crumbs and green onions. Spoon mixture onto open face French bread. Sprinkle with cheese and place into 350 degree oven for 10 minutes until cheese has melted.

Crabmeat Dip

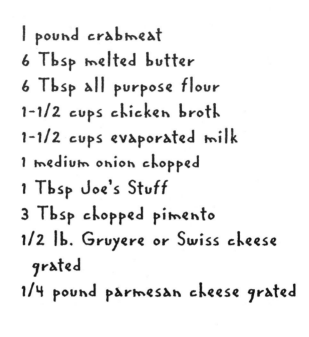

1 pound crabmeat
6 Tbsp melted butter
6 Tbsp all purpose flour
1-1/2 cups chicken broth
1-1/2 cups evaporated milk
1 medium onion chopped
1 Tbsp Joe's Stuff
3 Tbsp chopped pimento
1/2 lb. Gruyere or Swiss cheese
   grated
1/4 pound parmesan cheese grated

Drain and flake crabmeat, set aside. Combine butter and flour over low heat. Blend until smooth. Combine chicken broth and milk, gradually adding to flour mixture. Cook, stirring constantly, until smooth and thickened. Stir in onion, seasoning, pimento, cheese and crabmeat; heat until cheese melts. Serve warm and with crackers.

Shrimp Butter

1 pound cooked, cleaned shrimp
1 clove garlic
1/2 pound butter
fresh tarragon leaves

With the food processor, blend butter till smooth, add garlic and tarragon, blending until smooth again. Take shrimp and add to butter mixture, blending till shrimp are diced fine. Refrigerate till needed.

Spread at room temperature on canapés, crackers.

Pecan Cheese Crackers

1 pound sharp cheddar cheese,
  grated
2 sticks butter
3 cups flour
several dashes cayenne
2 cups finely chopped pecans

Using a food processor, cream butter and cheese together until well blended. Add flour and pepper, mix thoroughly. Pour into bowl and add chopped nuts, stirring well. Shape into rolls, then refrigerate. Slice the rolls about 1/4 inch thick and bake like cookies in 350 degree oven for 15 to 20 minutes. Do not brown.

13

Oysters Gigi

12 strips of bacon

3 eggs

2 dozen fresh shucked oysters, drained

12 ounces beer (not dark)

2 tsp salt

2 cups flour

1 tsp ground red pepper

2 cups seasoned Italian bread crumbs

1 tsp ground black pepper

1/2 tsp ground white pepper

vegetable oil for deep-frying

Halve the bacon slices and fry until transparent-about 2 minutes. Wrap a half strip of bacon around each oyster, secure with a toothpick. In a small bowl, mix together the salt and peppers; set aside. In a separate bowl, beat together the eggs and beer and half of the salt-pepper mixture. Mix together the flour and the remaining pepper mixture, place in a large flat pan. Place the bread crumbs in another large flat pan. Pour oil into a Dutch oven or other large heavy pot, heating oil to 375 degrees. Roll the bacon-wrapped oysters in the seasoned flour to coat them well, then dip into beer batter, stirring to coat, then roll them in bread crumbs. Deep-fry oysters in hot oil until browned, 2-3 minutes. Do not overcrowd. Drain on paper towels.

Stuffed Mushrooms

12 large mushrooms
1 cup bread crumbs
1 medium onion
1 Tbsp + dash Worcestershire
1 medium bell pepper
1 Tbsp + dash Tabasco
1 celery rib
1 Tbsp salt
1 cup (1/2) pound butter
1-1/2 tsp ground red pepper
1 pound crab meat
1 tsp black pepper
1/4 cup plus 3 Tbsp
   lemon juice
1 tsp white pepper
1/4 cup plus 2 Tbsp chopped
   green onions
1/4 cup plus 2 Tbsp chopped
   parsley
2 Tbsp vermouth

Remove the stems from mushrooms. Wipe the caps. Chop the onion, bell pepper, and celery fine and sauté in 1/4 pound of butter until soft. Stir in the crab meat and 1/4 cup

of the lemon juice and simmer for 10 minutes. Add 2 Tbsp each of the green onions and parsley, all the bread crumbs and a dash each of Worcestershire and Tabasco sauce. Simmer 4 - 5 minutes more, stirring often. Season with salt and pepper to taste. Remove dressing from heat and let cool. Stuff the mushroom caps generously with the dressing and place in a single layer in a shallow ovenproof dish. Melt the remaining 1/4 pound butter and add the remaining 3 Tbsp lemon juice and 1 tablespoon each of Worcestershire and Tabasco sauce, and vermouth. Simmer together for 1 minute, pour over the mushrooms, and bake in a preheated 350 degree oven for 15 minutes, or broil at 450 for 5 minutes.

Oyster Pockets

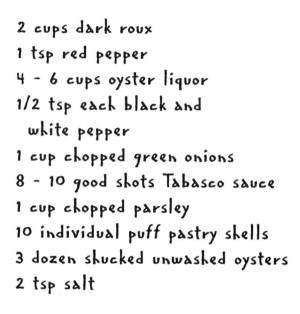

2 cups dark roux

1 tsp red pepper

4 - 6 cups oyster liquor

1/2 tsp each black and
white pepper

1 cup chopped green onions

8 - 10 good shots Tabasco sauce

1 cup chopped parsley

10 individual puff pastry shells

3 dozen shucked unwashed oysters

2 tsp salt

Warm the roux over low heat in a black iron skillet. Stir as much of the oyster liquor into the roux without it becoming too liquified. The mixture will become fluffy, like a mousse. Raise the heat to medium-high and add the green onions, parsley, oysters, and seasonings. Stir continuously, until the oysters curl around the edges. The mixture should be as thick as a chicken stew. You can always add a little more oyster water if it becomes too thick. Taste for seasoning, as the seasoning is the key to making the sauce. Spoon into pastry shells and serve hot.

Marinated Crab Fingers

1 pound crab fingers
1/2 cup olive oil
Juice of 3 lemons
2 tsp balsamic vinegar
1 Tbsp fresh basil, or
  1 tsp dry
1 tsp salt
2 tsp fresh thyme, or
  1/2 tsp dry
1 tsp ground black pepper
1 Tbsp chopped parsley
1/2 cup chopped garlic

Place crab fingers in a large bowl. Mix together the remaining ingredients and pour over. Stir well, cover and refrigerate several hours or overnight. If using crab fingers left over from a crab boil, do not season till you taste.

Shrimp Remoulade

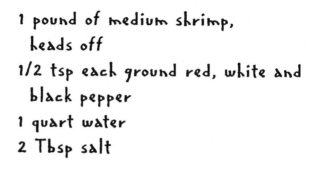

1 pound of medium shrimp,
   heads off
1/2 tsp each ground red, white and
   black pepper
1 quart water
2 Tbsp salt

Peel and devein the shrimp. Bring the water, salt, and peppers to a full boil in a medium saucepan over high heat. Drop in the shrimp and stir. Continue to cook over high heat for 2-3 minutes, stirring often, until the shrimp are pink and firm. Do not bring back to a boil. Drain the shrimp and cool them quickly in a bowl with ice.

Remoulade Sauce

1 cup olive oil
1-1/2 tsp salt
1 cup vinegar
1/2 cup white horseradish
1-1/3 cup Creole mustard
1/4 cup mayonnaise
1/3 cup paprika

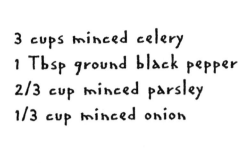

3 cups minced celery
1 Tbsp ground black pepper
2/3 cup minced parsley
1/3 cup minced onion

In a large mixing bowl, combine the olive oil, vinegar, mustard, paprika, pepper, salt, horseradish and mayonnaise. Add the celery, parsley, and onion, mixing well. When you are ready to serve, place the shrimp in a mixing bowl, add a generous amount of the remoulade sauce and mix well. Serve on a bed of lettuce.

Stuffed Artichokes

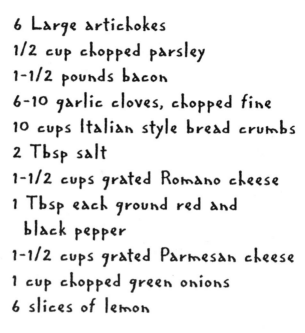

6 Large artichokes
1/2 cup chopped parsley
1-1/2 pounds bacon
6-10 garlic cloves, chopped fine
10 cups Italian style bread crumbs
2 Tbsp salt
1-1/2 cups grated Romano cheese
1 Tbsp each ground red and
   black pepper
1-1/2 cups grated Parmesan cheese
1 cup chopped green onions
6 slices of lemon

Slice off the pointed leaf ends of the artichokes. Slice off the bottom stem - to sit artichoke up straight. Fry the bacon until very crisp, drain thoroughly, and crumble fine by hand into a bowl. Mix in the bread crumbs, cheeses, green onions, parsley, garlic, salt and peppers. Spread the leaves of each artichoke as much as possible and pack in a generous amount of stuffing around them, then tap the artichokes lightly to let loose stuffing fall into the pan. Stand them in a roasting pan just large enough to hold a single layer. Add water to a depth of 1/2 the height of the artichokes. Pour a generous amount of olive oil over each artichoke, letting it seep in. Top each with a slice of lemon. Cover the artichokes, and steam over low heat until the leaves pull off easily (at least one hour). Check water level after about 25 minutes and add more if needed.

Fried Crawfish

3 eggs
2 tsp each ground black
  & white pepper
12 ounces beer
2 cups milk
oil for deep frying
2 cups all-purpose flour
2 pounds peeled crawfish tails
2 Tbsp salt
2 tsp ground red pepper

In a large bowl, beat together the eggs, beer, and milk. Place the flour in a wide shallow bowl. Mix together the salt and peppers and stir half into each bowl. Heat at least 3 inches of oil to 375 degrees in a deep fryer or large heavy pot. Pour the crawfish into the beer batter and mix well to coat. Remove about a quarter of the crawfish from the batter, using a slotted spoon to allow the excess batter to drain off, and dredge them in the flour mixture. Place them in a fry basket and shake basket to knock off excess flour. Fry the crawfish in basket until they are firm and golden, about 2 - 3 minutes. Drain on paper toweling. Repeat the dredging and frying process three times or until all crawfish are cooked.

Soups
&
Gumbos

Corn & Crab Bisque

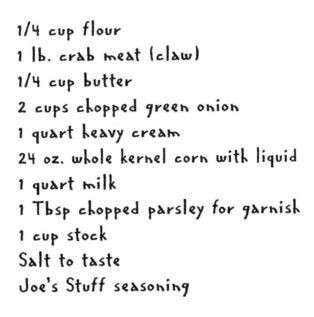

1/4 cup flour
1 lb. crab meat (claw)
1/4 cup butter
2 cups chopped green onion
1 quart heavy cream
24 oz. whole kernel corn with liquid
1 quart milk
1 Tbsp chopped parsley for garnish
1 cup stock
Salt to taste
Joe's Stuff seasoning

Combine milk, heavy cream and stock. Bring to a boil, then reduce to a simmer for about 10 - 12 minutes. Make a roux with equal parts of butter and flour to desired color; add in to your simmering pot. Stir in your corn with liquid, crab-meat and simmer for another 5 minutes.

Gradually add in half your green onions, salt and seasoning to taste.
*NOTE: use the other half of green onions and parsley for garnish.

Chicken & Andouille Gumbo

1 cup oil
1 Tbsp chopped garlic
1 chicken, cut up and boned
8 cups stock or flavored water
1-1/2 lbs. andouille
2 cups chopped green onions
1 cup flour
cooked rice
TRINITY: (next three items)
4 cups chopped onions
2 cups chopped celery
2 cups chopped green pepper
Joe's Stuff seasoning
File

Season and brown chicken in oil (lard, bacon drippings) over medium heat. Add sausage to pot and sauté with chicken. Remove both from pot.

Make a roux with equal parts of oil (must be free of food particles to avoid burning) and flour to desired color. Add onions,

celery, green pepper. Add garlic to the mixture and stir continuously. After vegetables reach desired tenderness, return chicken and sausage to pot and cook with vegetables, continuing to stir frequently. Gradually stir in liquid and bring to a boil. Reduce heat to simmer and cook for an hour or more. Season to taste with seasoning.

Approximately 10 minutes before serving, add green onions. Serve gumbo over rice or without rice, accompanied by French bread.

File may be placed on the table for individuals to add to their gumbo if they wish. 1/4 to 1/2 tsp per serving is recommended.

Seafood Gumbo

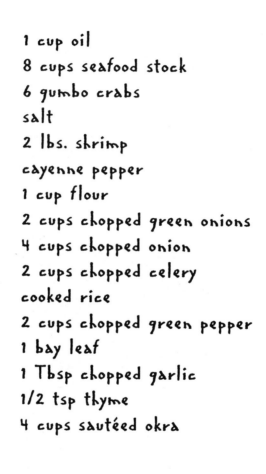

1 cup oil
8 cups seafood stock
6 gumbo crabs
salt
2 lbs. shrimp
cayenne pepper
1 cup flour
2 cups chopped green onions
4 cups chopped onion
2 cups chopped celery
cooked rice
2 cups chopped green pepper
1 bay leaf
1 Tbsp chopped garlic
1/2 tsp thyme
4 cups sautéed okra

Make a roux with equal parts oil (must be free of food particles to avoid burning) and flour to desired color (brown to dark brown.) Add onions, celery, green pepper, and later garlic to roux, and stir continu-

ously until vegetables reach desired tenderness.

Gradually stir in liquid and bring to a boil. Add crabs and reduce to simmer and cook for an hour or more. Season to taste.

Approximately 10 minutes before serving, add green onions, shrimp and sautéed okra. Gumbo may be served over rice. Adding sherry at the table is also an option.

Shrimp & Artichoke Soup

24 oz. quartered artichokes
1/4 cup plus 1 Tbsp flour
1 quart strong chicken stock
1 qt. heavy cream
1 Tbsp chopped parsley (for garnish)
2 cups chopped green onions
1 Tbsp thyme leaves
1/4 cup melted butter
1 lb. medium shrimp, peeled and deveined
1 Tbsp Joe's Stuff seasoning

Combine artichoke, chicken stock, 1/2 of the green onions, seasoning, thyme and bring to a boil. Reduce to a simmer for about 12 minutes.

Combine butter and flour for a light roux and add to simmering pot. Stir in heavy cream and simmer for 10 minutes. Add shrimp and simmer for 5 more minutes. Serve with freshly chopped green onions and parsley for garnish.

NOTE: There are 2 cups green onions total - 1 cup to put with other ingredients and one cup for garnish. The quart of strong chicken stock can be substituted by liquid drained from shrimp or liquid from artichokes.

Shrimp Bisque

1 cup flour
4 cups stock
1 cup butter
2 bay leaves
2 cups chopped onions
1/2 cup green onions
1 cup chopped celery
1/2 cup parsley
1 cup chopped green pepper
3 Tbsp Joe's Stuff seasoning
1 Tbsp garlic
2 lbs. shrimp (peeled)
2 oz. tomato paste
cooked rice

In your pot cook butter and flour making a roux to the color of dark peanut butter. Add onion, celery, green pepper and tomato paste. Stir these ingredients into your roux to stop the cooking process. Pour in your stock and return to heat stirring to smooth the roux mixture into the stock. Add garlic, bay leaves and seasoning.

Cook the bisque on a medium heat for 15 minutes, letting the flavors blend together. Add shrimp, cooking for 5 minutes or until shrimp are done. Sprinkle in green onions and parsley just prior to serving. Serve over cooked rice.

You may prepare this ahead of time, without adding the shrimp till ready to serve.

Oyster and Artichoke Soup

2 quarts heavy cream
1/4 tsp salt
1 pint oyster liquor or oyster water
1/4 tsp each ground black, red
    and white pepper,
2 cans of quartered artichoke
    hearts
1 tsp each dried thyme and basil
2 dozen fresh oysters, shucked
1/2 cup chopped parsley
1/2 cup chopped green onions

Place heavy cream into a 4 - 6 quart stockpot, bring to a boil over medium heat and reduce to 1-1/2 quarts, add oyster liquor and continue cooking. Add the herbs, salt and peppers and let simmer slowly, stirring often with a whisk to keep the soup smooth and the cream from curdling, about 30 minutes. Add the artichoke hearts.

Just before serving, add the oysters, parsley, and green onions to the soup and let simmer just until the edges of the oysters curl, 4 - 5 minutes. Serve immediately.

Duck and Oyster Gumbo

3 Tbsp salt
6 quarts duck or chicken stock
1 Tbsp ground black pepper
2 large onions, chopped fine
1 Tbsp ground red pepper
2 large bell peppers, chopped fine
2 tsp ground white pepper
2 celery ribs, chopped fine
2 ducks, 3 - 4 pounds each, cut into serving pieces
3 1/2 dozen oysters with water
1 cup chopped green onions
1 cup flour
1 cup finely chopped parsley
1 cup oil
2 - 3 cups dark roux

In a small bowl, mix together the salt and ground peppers; set aside. Place the duck pieces in a large bowl, add a third of the salt-pepper mixture and rub in well. Place the flour in a large flat pan. Add 2 teaspoons of the salt-pepper mixture and

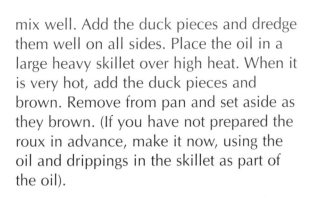

mix well. Add the duck pieces and dredge them well on all sides. Place the oil in a large heavy skillet over high heat. When it is very hot, add the duck pieces and brown. Remove from pan and set aside as they brown. (If you have not prepared the roux in advance, make it now, using the oil and drippings in the skillet as part of the oil).

Place the stock in a large stockpot and add the onions, bell peppers, celery, remaining salt and pepper, and the roux. Bring to a boil over medium-high heat, reduce heat and let simmer for 1 hour. Add the duck and let simmer until the duck is very tender. Add the oysters 10 minutes before you want to serve. You may want to de-grease the gumbo before you add the oysters. To do this, let gumbo sit and fat will rise to top. Skim off, then return to fire and add oysters. Taste for seasoning.

This is to be served over rice and with French bread.

Redfish Courtbouillon

4 cups medium - dark roux
3 bell peppers, chopped
1 can (15oz.) tomato sauce
1 rib celery, chopped
3 cups peeled, roughly chopped
    fresh tomatoes
1 Tbsp salt
2 tsp ground black pepper
1 redfish, 6 - 10 pounds
8 quarts water
1-1/2 tsp white pepper
3 large carrots
2 tsp red pepper
3 celery ribs
6 shots Tabasco sauce
3 onions, chopped coarse
1 cup chopped green onions
1/2 cup chopped hard-boiled eggs
1 cup chopped parsley

Warm the roux in a well-seasoned skillet as large and heavy as you have. Raise the heat and add the tomato sauce and tomatoes, stirring to mix thoroughly. Cook over

medium-high heat, stirring frequently, until the oil begins to separate out around the edges (Dark mahogany color.) Remove from heat and cool.

Fillet the fish. Cut the bones in 3-inch sections and place with the head in large stockpot (10-quart). Add water, carrots and the 3 celery ribs and bring to a boil. Boil slowly, uncovered for 1-1/2 hour. Stock should reduce to about 6 quarts. Strain well and return the stock to pot.
Skim off the fat that has separated from the roux and discard. Place the stock over medium-high heat and add the chopped onions, bell peppers and celery. When it boils, gradually stir in enough roux to reach a consistency halfway between a stew and a gumbo. Add the salt and peppers, and hot sauce. Reduce heat and let boil slowly for 45 minutes to 1 hour, stirring occasionally.

Cut the fish into serving pieces and add to the courtbouillon. Cook 5 - 10 minutes more. Remove from heat and let stand 5 minutes more. Skim off any grease from the surface and discard. Stir in the green onions and parsley and serve immediately over rice in bowls. Garnish with chopped eggs.

Turtle Soup

1/4 cup salt
1 1/2 cups fresh or frozen
   turtle meat
6 cups chicken or veal stock
2 cloves garlic, chopped
2 bay leaves
1 pinch dried whole thyme
3 Tbsp tomato paste
1/2 cup chopped celery
1 cup chopped green onions
1/2 cup chopped onions
1 Tbsp chopped fresh parsley
2 lemons, cut in half
3 Tbsp sherry
2 eggs, hard-boiled and chopped
Salt and white pepper to taste
2 Tbsp roux, if desired

To cook the turtle meat, bring 4 quarts of water to a boil in a large pot and simmer the meat for 45 minutes. Drain off the water and chop the meat coarsely. Set aside until needed.

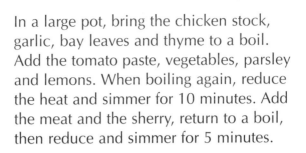

In a large pot, bring the chicken stock, garlic, bay leaves and thyme to a boil. Add the tomato paste, vegetables, parsley and lemons. When boiling again, reduce the heat and simmer for 10 minutes. Add the meat and the sherry, return to a boil, then reduce and simmer for 5 minutes.

Add the eggs. Season to taste with salt and pepper. Thicken if desired by adding small amounts of roux. Serve in soup bowls, preferably with a final splash of sherry.

NOTE: Naturally, the key to making turtle soup is ground turtle meat, which is available in many meat markets and especially in small, ethnic groceries. Ground veal works well as a substitute, but you can't call it turtle soup with no turtle in the pot.

Brunch

French Style Eggs

1/2 cup (1 stick) butter
4 medium onions, thinly sliced
12 hard-boiled eggs
Salt
Black pepper
2 cups light cream, heated
3 Tbsp grated Swiss or
  Parmesan cheese

Melt 4 Tbsps of butter in large skillet, add the onions, and 1 cup water. Bring to a boil, reduce heat to moderate and cook until all water has boiled away and the onions are tender and transparent. Add more water if necessary. Peel and slice the eggs rather thin. Generously butter a medium-size ovenproof serving dish. Make alternate layers of the eggs and onions, starting with the eggs; sprinkle each layer with salt and pepper.

Heat 3 Tbsps butter in a saucepan. Stir in flour and cook over medium heat, stirring constantly for 2 - 3 minutes, not browning. Stir in the cream and cook whipping constantly over moderate heat until sauce has thickened, 8 - 10 minutes. Pour sauce over eggs and onions. Sprinkle with grated cheese and dot with remaining butter. Preheat oven to 400 degrees. Just heat up enough to brown top of casserole and warm inside.

French Toast

3 eggs
1-1/2 cups milk
dash of nutmeg
dash of cinnamon
vanilla to taste
6 thick slices Texas toast

Beat eggs to a creamy texture, add in milk and mix together. Add in nutmeg, cinnamon and vanilla to taste. Dip toast into mixture, and place toast into a non-stick skillet browning on one side, 2 - 3 minutes. Repeat process on other side. Serve with powdered sugar or syrup.

Quiche Lorraine
(Bacon-cheese pie)

9" unbaked pastry shell
1/4 pound sliced bacon
1 cup shredded cheddar cheese
3 eggs
2/3 cup (6 oz. can) evaporated milk
1-1/3 cups milk
1 tsp salt
dash black pepper
dash cayenne pepper

Fry bacon until crisp. Drain. Crumble into pastry shell. Arrange shredded cheese over bacon. Beat eggs slightly, along with both milks and seasoning.

Pour mixture over cheese. Bake 400 degrees for 25 - 30 minutes or until knife inserted 2 inches from edge comes out clean. Do not overbake. Cut in wedges and serve hot.

Our Eggs

2 or 3 eggs
1/4 pound diced andouille sausage
2 Tbsp whipping cream
a few Tbsp sweet butter

Melt butter in a warm heavy frying pan. Add sausage and cream, then break the eggs into the pan. Mix slowly with a spoon (do not beat), and let the eggs warm with the pan, gradually pulling in the sides as the eggs cook. The eggs are done when they are lightly blended and set. Herbs or grated cheese may be added halfway through the process.

Eggs Sardou

1-1/2 cups creamed spinach,
 piping hot
8 artichokes, boiled in salted water
 (or canned whole artichoke hearts)
8 eggs, poached
1 cup hollandaise sauce
1/2 cup chopped cooked ham

Remove the chokes from the artichokes
and leaves and fill each heart with
creamed spinach. Slip a poached egg on
top of the spinach and smooth each with
Hollandaise sauce. Sprinkle with a little
chopped ham and serve.

Muffaletta

1 round loaf Italian bread
6 slices Genoa-style salami
3 slices baked ham
3 slices Provolone cheese
3 slices Swiss cheese
3 slices Mortadella
4 Tbsp olive salad

Layer salami, ham, cheeses, mortadella on bread. Top with olive salad. Be sure to brush both sides of the bread with the "juice" from the olive salad.

Can be heated briefly, just long enough to soften the cheeses.

Olive Salad

1/2 cup pimento-stuffed olives
1/2 cup black olives, cut
1/2 cup finely chopped celery
1/4 cup finely chopped carrots

1/4 cup finely chopped cauliflower
  (optional)
1 Tbsp chopped green pepper
1 Tbsp parsley
1 Tbsp minced garlic
1 Tbsp minced onion
1 cup olive oil
1/3 cup vegetable oil
1/2 tsp each: salt, oregano,
  coarse black pepper

Mix all together in a quart jar. Olive salad
keeps well refrigerated

Red Beans & Rice

1 large onion
1 pound red kidney beans
1 cup celery
3 qts stock
3 Tbsp oil
1/2 lb. smoked sausage or
   ham chunks
2 Tbsp garlic
1 bay leaf
2 Tbsp Joe's Stuff seasoning
1 cup parsley
6 cups cooked rice

Soak beans in water overnight to soften. Drain beans and place in pot with stock on low fire. Coat a skillet with oil and sauté onions, celery, smoked sausage or ham chunks for 10 minutes. Empty contents of skillet into pot with beans and bring to boil. Add garlic, bay leaf, and seasoning. Reduce to a simmer for 3 hours or until beans are creamy. Add more stock if necessary so pot does not become dry. Stir in parsley, serve over cooked rice.

Creole Grillades and Grits

2 pounds round steak, 1/2inch thick

1 tsp sugar

1 cup flour seasoned with salt and pepper

1 bay leaf

4 Tbsp oil

1/4 tsp each thyme, basil and oregano

2 onions, chopped

1 bell pepper, chopped

salt and pepper to taste

2 ribs celery, chopped

1 Tbsp Worcestershire

3 cloves garlic, crushed

1-1/2 cup beef broth

1 (10oz.) can Ro-tel tomatoes with green chilies, chopped

1/2 cup dry red wine

2 Tbsp each chopped parsley and green onions

3 Tbsp tomato paste

Trim and cut steak into serving - size pieces. Sprinkle liberally with seasoned flour. Beat with tenderizing mallet until flour is pounded in and meat is thin. Brown meat in oil in large skillet. Remove from skillet and set aside. Add onion, bell pepper, celery and garlic to skillet. Sauté until wilted. Add tomatoes, tomato paste, and sugar. Simmer 4 minutes. Add bay leaf, thyme, basil, oregano, salt and pepper to taste. Add Worcestershire, broth, wine, parsley and onion tops. Bring to a boil. Reduce heat, add meat. Cover, simmer over low heat 30 - 40 minutes until meat is tender and gravy is thick. Serve over hot grits.

Pork Medallions

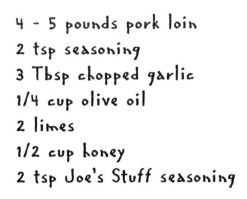

4 - 5 pounds pork loin
2 tsp seasoning
3 Tbsp chopped garlic
1/4 cup olive oil
2 limes
1/2 cup honey
2 tsp Joe's Stuff seasoning

Preheat oven to 350 degrees.

Place pork in a bowl and rub with olive oil. Season pork with Joe's Stuff. Place pork in a roasting pan and place the chopped garlic over the top, then squeeze the two limes over the pork. Cook pork 1 -1/2 to 2 hours until the inside of the pork reaches 160-180 degrees. When you take the pork out of the oven pour the honey over the top and let set for approximately 10 minutes. Cut into 1/4 to 1/2 inch medallions.

Braised Pork Chops with Tomato and Garlic Sauce

4 Tbsp olive oil

1/2 cup dry red wine

6 center-cut loin pork chops,
  cut 1 to 1-1/2 inches thick

1 cup drained canned tomatoes
  pureed through a sieve or mill

1 tsp finely chopped garlic

1 Tbsp tomato paste

1/2 tsp dried oregano,
  crumbled

1/2 pound green peppers
  seeded and cut into 1/4" strips

1/4 tsp dried thyme,
  crumbled

1/2 bay leaf

1/2 pound fresh mushrooms,
  sliced and quartered

1/2 tsp salt

In a heavy 10 - 12 inch skillet, heat 2 tablespoons of olive oil until a light haze forms over it. Brown the chops in this oil for 2 to 3 minutes on each side and transfer them to a plate. Pour off almost all of the fat. In remaining fat cook the garlic, oregano, thyme, bay leaf and salt for 30 seconds, stirring constantly. Add the wine and boil briskly to reduce it to about 1/4 cup, scraping in any bits of meat or herbs in the pan. Stir in the tomatoes and tomato paste and return the chops to the skillet. Baste with the sauce, cover, and simmer over low heat, basting once or twice for 40 minutes.

Meanwhile, heat the remaining oil in another large skillet. Fry the green peppers in the oil for about 5 minutes, stirring frequently. Add the mushrooms and toss them with the peppers for a minute or two, then transfer them to the pan with the pork chops. Cover and simmer for 5 minutes. Simmer uncovered, stirring occasionally, for 10 minutes longer, until the pork and vegetables are tender and the sauce is thick enough to coat a spoon heavily. (If the sauce is too thin, remove the chops and vegetables and boil the sauce down over high heat, stirring constantly.) Serve over pasta or grits.

Cajun Sauce Piquant

3 - 1/2 lbs. fish fillets
1/3 cup oil
2 cups chopped onions
1 cup chopped sweet pepper
1 cup chopped celery
5 cloves garlic, minced
1 (14-1/2 oz.) can whole tomatoes
2 (6 oz.) cans tomato paste
2 (8 oz.) cans tomato sauce
1 cup mushrooms, chopped
2 Tbsp Worcestershire sauce
1/4 Tbsp basil
2 bay leaves
4 cups hot stock
2 Tbsp minced parsley
2 Tbsp green onion
6 thin slices lemon
1/2 cup Joe's Stuff seasoning
1 Tbsp brown sugar

In a large pot, sauté onions and celery until lightly brown. Add sweet pepper, whole tomatoes, tomato sauce, tomato paste, mushrooms, sugar, basil, and bay leaves. Cover and cook over very low heat, about 2 hours, stirring and adding water as needed. Stir in garlic, stock, Worcestershire sauce, parsley, green onion, lemon, and seasoning. Cook for 30 minutes longer. Fry fish in a little margarine and add to tomato mixture. Simmer for 10 minutes.

Seafood

Crabmeat au Gratin

1 stalk celery, chopped fine
1 large onion, chopped
1/4 pound butter
1/2 cup all purpose flour
1 can evaporated milk (13 oz)
2 egg yolks
1 tsp salt
1/4 tsp red pepper
1/4 tsp black pepper
1 lb. white crabmeat
1/2 lb. grated cheddar cheese

Sauté onion, celery in butter until wilted. Blend flour in well with mixture. Pour in milk gradually, stirring constantly. Add egg yolks, salt, red and black pepper. Cook for 5 minutes. Put crabmeat in bowl suitable for mixing. Pour sauce over crabmeat. Blend well. Pour into lightly greased casserole. Sprinkle with grated cheddar cheese. Bake at 375 degrees for 15 minutes or until lightly brown.

Oysters Bienville

4 Tbsp butter
8 small shallots, finely chopped
2 Tbsp flour
1 cup chicken broth or fish stock
1 cup cooked shrimp, finely
  chopped
1 (7 oz.) can mushroom pieces,
  chopped
2 egg yolks
1/2 cup white wine
salt and pepper to taste
1/2 cup bread crumbs
2 Tbsp Parmesan cheese
2 dozen oysters on half shell
paprika

Heat butter in fry pan, add shallots and
sauté until soft. Add flour and stir until
lightly browned. Stir in chicken broth or
fish stock, stirring until blended. Add
shrimp and mushrooms. Beat egg yolks
with wine, and add to mixture, stirring
until blended and slightly thickened.
Remove from heat and season to taste with

salt and pepper. Remove oysters from shells and set aside. Scrub shells thoroughly. Arrange six shells on each of four pie pans half filled with rock salt. Heat in a 450 degree oven for 10 minutes. Remove pans from oven, place oysters in shells and top each with a spoonful of the prepared mixture. Combine bread crumbs and Parmesan cheese and sprinkle atop mixture, then lightly sprinkle with paprika. Bake in a 450 degree oven 15 minutes or until tips are lightly browned

Oysters Rockefeller

4 large lettuce leaves
4 ounces frozen spinach
2 Tbsp chopped parsley
2 shallots
1 rib celery
4 Tbsp butter
juice of half a lemon
1 tsp anchovy paste
1/2 tsp Worcestershire sauce
2 Tbsp bread crumbs
1 Tbsp Herbsaint or Pernod
dash hot sauce
1/2 tsp salt
1/8 tsp pepper
2 dozen oysters on the half shell

Coarsely chop lettuce, spinach, parsley, shallots and celery and put through food chopper along with remaining ingredients (except oysters). Blend well. Remove oysters from shells and set aside. Scrub shells thoroughly. Arrange six shells on each of

four pie pans half filled with rock salt.
Heat in a 450 degree oven for 10 minutes.
Remove pans from oven, place oysters in
shells and top each with a spoonful of the
prepared mixture. Return to oven and
bake 20 to 25 minutes, or until lightly
browned.

Shrimp Mosca

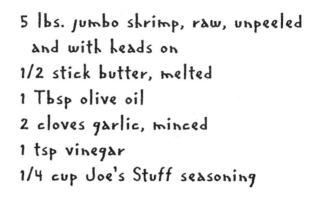

5 lbs. jumbo shrimp, raw, unpeeled
   and with heads on
1/2 stick butter, melted
1 Tbsp olive oil
2 cloves garlic, minced
1 tsp vinegar
1/4 cup Joe's Stuff seasoning

Wash shrimp thoroughly. Drain and dry well with paper towels. Combine remaining ingredients, pour over shrimp and allow to marinate. Cover and refrigerate overnight. When ready to cook, heat a heavy pot or Dutch oven and add shrimp with marinade. Cook over medium high heat until bubbly, then lower heat and simmer covered 25 - 30 minutes until shrimp are tender. Serve to folks with sleeves rolled up and bibs on, and pass lots of French bread for dipping in sauce.

Fried Oysters

3 dozen large oysters (2 to 2-1/2 lbs.)
salt and pepper
2 cups cracker crumbs,
  crushed fine
2 eggs, beaten
shortening

Drain oysters and press between absorbent paper. Season oysters with salt and pepper. Dip in cracker crumbs, then beaten egg and then cracker crumbs again. Fry in shortening until golden brown.

Crawfish Jambalaya

3 pounds crawfish tails
  (retain juice)
2 sticks of butter
2 Tbsp flour
6 onions, chopped
1/2 cup chopped parsley
1/2 cup chopped green onions
salt, black pepper and red pepper
  to taste
3 cups cooked rice

Melt butter and add flour. Brown a little bit. Add onions and simmer until soft. Add juice from crawfish. Simmer a few more minutes and then add tails, parsley, green onions and seasoning. Cook 15 minutes. When ready to serve, stir cooked rice into mixture.

Frog Legs Provençal

18 pairs medium frog legs
1 qt. milk
flour
salt
freshly ground pepper
olive oil
3/4 cup (1-1/2 sticks) butter
lemon juice
6 large cloves of garlic, peeled
 and minced
1/2 cup parsley sprigs, minced
lemon wedges

Place the frog legs in large bowl and cover with milk. Season generously with salt and pepper. It will take several hours for legs to thaw, so you might as well do this in the morning. Thaw at room temperature. Fifteen minutes before dinner is to be served, lift the legs from the milk and dry on a clean dish towel. Mix up several tablespoons of flour with a good seasoning of salt and pepper in a large polyethylene

bag. Add the legs, shake until lightly coated. Heat enough olive oil in a large heavy skillet to make a light film on the bottom. When hot, sauté the legs a few at a time, until nicely brown and crisp all over, four to five minutes. Add more oil as it is needed. Lift from the pan to a heated platter and keep warm in oven.

While you fry the legs, cut the butter into pieces and heat in a second skillet over low heat. When hot, add minced garlic. The butter and the garlic will gradually turn a golden brown. Stir in lemon juice, salt and pepper to taste, then add parsley. Pour over the frog legs and serve at once with a lemon wedge garnish.

Shrimp and Spinach Delight

1 pound raw shrimp, shelled
and deveined
1/2 cup sliced celery
1/2 cup diagonally sliced
green onion
1 medium clove garlic, minced
2 Tbsp butter
1 can (10 1/2 oz) condensed cream
of mushroom soup
1/4 cup milk
1/8 tsp nutmeg
1 lb. spinach, cleaned
Chinese noodles, heated

In skillet, cook shrimp, celery, green onions, and garlic in butter till celery is tender. Stir in soup, milk and nutmeg, heat. Put in casserole, then top with spinach, cover and heat in oven at 350 degrees for about 10 minutes or until tender. Serve with noodles.

Crabmeat - Artichoke Casserole

3 Tbsp butter
3 Tbsp flour
1 tsp each salt and black pepper
1/8 tsp dry mustard
1-1/2 cup milk
1/2 tsp Worcestershire
dash of Tabasco
1/2 cup Parmesan cheese
4 hard boiled eggs
1 can artichoke hearts (1 lb.)
1 can (3/4 pound) claw crabmeat

Melt butter, stir in flour, salt, pepper and mustard. Cook until smooth. Gradually add milk and cook until thickened while stirring constantly. Add Worcestershire, hot sauce and 1/4 cup cheese. Stir in eggs, artichokes and crabmeat. Pour into 1-1/2 quart casserole, top with remaining cheese. Bake in 350 degree oven for 30 minutes.

Shrimp Stuffed Mirlitons

12 medium mirlitons
2 cups chopped onions
1 cup sweet pepper, chopped
1 cup celery, chopped
4 cloves of garlic, chopped
6 cups raw shrimp, minced
1 gallon water
cooking oil
salt and pepper to taste

Cut mirlitons in half. Boil for 20 minutes in water. Remove seed and scrape out the pulp, leaving 1/4 inch rind. Mash. Sauté onions, pepper, celery and garlic in oil until brown. Add raw shrimp. Cook for 30 minutes. Add mashed mirlitons to shrimp mixture. Cook for 20 minutes. Lightly stuff the skin. Wrap in foil. Bake at 400 degrees for 45 minutes, open top of foil and bake 15 minutes more.

Pasta William

1 cup heavy cream
1/4 cup chopped green onions
2 Tbsp butter
1 pound pasta of your choice
1 lb. cooked crawfish tails
1 Tbsp Joe's Stuff seasoning

Sauté cooked crawfish tails with butter for 3 - 5 minutes. Add heavy cream, seasoning and cooked pasta. Bring to a boil, then reduce heat to a simmer until cream reduces and coats pasta. Garnish with chopped green onions.

Crawfish Cornbread Dressing

3 lbs. crawfish tails
2 (10-ounce) cans seafood
   base or broth
2 sticks margarine
4 cups corn bread
4 chopped onions
1/2 cup chopped green onion
4 stalks chopped celery
Joe's Stuff seasoning to taste
2 cloves garlic, minced

In Dutch oven, sauté crawfish tails in margarine. Add onions, celery and garlic. Sauté five minutes; add bouillon. Bring to boil and simmer for 10 minutes. Mix in 4 cups corn bread and 1/2 cup green onions. Season to taste.

Crawfish Boil

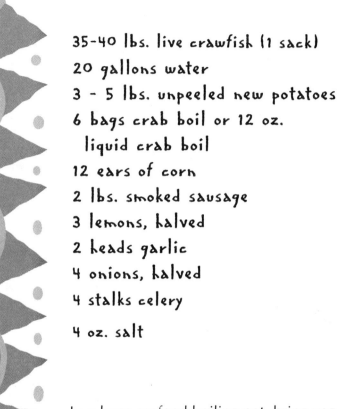

35-40 lbs. live crawfish (1 sack)

20 gallons water

3 - 5 lbs. unpeeled new potatoes

6 bags crab boil or 12 oz.
liquid crab boil

12 ears of corn

2 lbs. smoked sausage

3 lemons, halved

2 heads garlic

4 onions, halved

4 stalks celery

4 oz. salt

In a large seafood boiling pot, bring vegetables and seasonings to a boil for about 15 minutes. Add potatoes, corn and smoked sausage. Boil for another 10 minutes. Add crawfish. Bring back to a boil. Boil crawfish 10 minutes. Turn off heat. Let soak for 20 - 30 minutes. Drain and cool. Spread on large tables lined with newspaper. Peel and eat.

Crawfish Pie

1 lb. crawfish tails
3 Tbsp flour
1-1/2 sticks butter
1 pint heavy cream
1 cup onions, chopped
salt, black and red pepper
  to taste
1 cup chopped celery
2 cups white wine
1 cup chopped green pepper
14 small pastry shells, warmed
1/2 cup chopped parsley

In a skillet, sauté onions, celery, peppers and parsley in butter. Blend in flour and gradually add wine and cream, stirring constantly to make a thick sauce. Blend crawfish tails into cream sauce. Season to taste with salt, black and red pepper. Place mixture in pastry shells.

New Orleans-Style Barbecued Shrimp

1 lb. butter
5 oz beer
2 Tbsp Joe's Stuff seasoning
1 tsp lemon juice
1/4 cup Worcestershire sauce
1 tsp chopped garlic
3 - 4 lbs. shrimp, heads and
  shells on

Melt 3/4 lb. butter in skillet, and sauté garlic, shrimp and seasoning. Cook for 2 - 3 minutes. Add beer, lemon juice and Worcestershire sauce. Cook for 3 - 6 minutes, until shrimp are cooked and liquid thickens. Add remaining butter and shake pan until butter is melted and mixture creams out. Serve with plenty of French bread to sop up sauce.

Fried Soft Shell Crabs

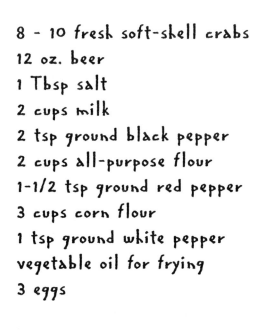

8 - 10 fresh soft-shell crabs
12 oz. beer
1 Tbsp salt
2 cups milk
2 tsp ground black pepper
2 cups all-purpose flour
1-1/2 tsp ground red pepper
3 cups corn flour
1 tsp ground white pepper
vegetable oil for frying
3 eggs

Clean the crabs: lift the pointed sides and remove the lungs or gills on each side with a small sharp knife, then remove the mud pockets located between the eyes. In a small bowl, mix together the salt and peppers. In a separate bowl, beat together the eggs, beer, milk, and one third of the salt-pepper mixture. Divide the rest of the salt-pepper mixture equally between the flour and corn flour, and place each mixture in a separate large flat pan. Pour oil into a Dutch oven or other large heavy pot

to a depth of a least 3 inches. Place over medium high heat and heat to 350 degrees.

Working with three or four crabs at a time, dredge them gently in flour on both sides, then dip in beer batter, then dredge in the corn flour and place immediately in the hot oil. (Crabs have a high water content, so do not do too many at a time.) Fry the crabs until they are nicely browned, 4 - 5 minutes, turning once. Drain on paper toweling and served immediately.

Cajun Eggplant Dressing

2 lbs. eggplant

2 pound medium fresh shrimp, heads off

4 - 6 dashes Tabasco

4 cups water

1 tsp dry thyme

1 cup margarine

1 tsp dry basil

3 large onions, chopped

1/2 tsp dry oregano

2 celery ribs, chopped

1 pound crabmeat

2 medium bell peppers, chopped

1 cup chopped green onions

1-1/2 tsp ground red pepper

1 cup chopped parsley

1-1/2 tsp ground white pepper

grated Parmesan cheese

1-1/2 tsp ground black pepper

bread crumbs

1-1/2 Tbsp salt

Peel and devein the shrimp; set aside. Place the peels in a small saucepan and add the water. Bring to a boil and reduce by half over medium high heat, 15 - 20 minutes. Strain and set aside.

Melt the margarine over medium high heat in a Dutch oven or other large heavy pot and add the onions, peppers and celery. Cook the vegetables until they are very soft, stirring occasionally, 30 - 40 minutes. Meanwhile, peel the eggplants and cut them into 1 - inch cubes. Place them in a saucepan and add water to cover. Bring to a boil and boil slowly for a few minutes, just until tender. Drain. Puree until smooth in a food processor.

Add the eggplant, shrimp stock, seasonings and herbs to the vegetable mixture and return to a simmer. Cook over medium heat for 10 minutes, stirring occasionally. Add the shrimp and continue to cook over medium high heat just until the shrimp turn pink, 5 - 7 minutes. Add the crabmeat and cook just long enough to heat through. Remove from the heat and stir in the green onions and parsley. Spoon the hot dressing into a casserole or individual ramekins. Sprinkle generously with Parmesan cheese and bread crumbs - glaze under the broiler for a couple of minutes.

Crawfish Étouffée

2 cups (1 pound) butter
2 oz. crawfish fat
3 large onions, chopped fine
1 cup water
2 bell peppers, chopped fine
2 pounds fresh crawfish tails
1 red bell pepper, chopped fine
1 cup finely chopped green onions
2 tsp salt
1/2 cup finely chopped parsley
3/4 tsp ground red pepper
1/2 tsp ground black and white
 pepper

Melt the butter in a Dutch oven or other large heavy pot, add the onions and bell peppers, and sauté over medium high heat. Brown well, being sure to scrape the bottom of the pot frequently to loosen any stuck particles. This process will take about 45 minutes.

Reduce the heat to medium low and add the salt, peppers, crawfish fat, and water. Stir well and let simmer 30 minutes more. (You can prepare the dish in advance to this point; about 30 minutes before serving, reheat the mixture over medium high heat.)

Raise the heat to medium, stir in the crawfish and cook for 10 minutes. Then add the green onions and parsley and let it cook for another 5 minutes. Place generous servings of hot cooked rice in the middle of large flat plates and spoon the crawfish around.

Fried Crawfish

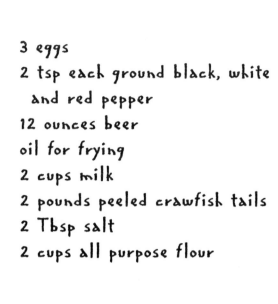

3 eggs
2 tsp each ground black, white
  and red pepper
12 ounces beer
oil for frying
2 cups milk
2 pounds peeled crawfish tails
2 Tbsp salt
2 cups all purpose flour

In a large bowl, beat together the eggs,
beer and milk. Place the flour in a wide
shallow bowl. Mix together the salt and
peppers and stir half into each bowl.
Heat at least 3 inches of oil to 375 degrees
in a deep fryer or large heavy pot. Coat
the crawfish with the batter, using a slotted
spoon to allow the excess batter to drain
off, and dredge them in the flour mixture.
Fry the crawfish in the basket until they
are firm and golden brown, 2 - 3 minutes.
Drain on paper toweling. Repeat the
dredging and frying process for the rest of
the crawfish.

Summer Crab Salad

1 dozen boiled crabs or 2 lbs. special
  white or lump crabmeat
2 cups olive oil
1/2 cup chopped rosemary
1/3 cup Joe's Stuff seasoning
1/2 cup chopped fresh garlic
1 cup chopped purple onion
Mixed greens
1 cup green onions
1 cup chopped parsley

Mix the olive oil and all the seasonings, purple onion and parsley. Take and clean crabs, opening each half. Put all cleaned crabs in a large bowl then pour the olive oil mixture in bowl and toss well. Cover and refrigerate overnight. Serve over salad.

Crab Stew Monteleone

1 cup olive oil
1-1/2 cups all purpose flour
1/2 lb. sweet green peppers, chopped
1 Tbsp minced garlic
1 tsp crushed red pepper
3 lbs. onions chopped
3 stalks celery, chopped
1 dozen large blue crabs
salt to taste
chopped parsley
chopped green onions

Put olive oil in large iron pot; heat thoroughly and stir in flour. Cook over very low leat for about 30 minutes stirring constantly so flour does not brown. Add green pepper, garlic, red pepper, onion and celery. Cook slowly for about 20 minutes, stirring once or twice. Add crabs which have been cleaned and cut into halves (do not discard the crab fat). Stir well, add salt to taste and cover pot. Do not add water at any time, cook slowly for 30 minutes, then add crab fat and meat from claws. Simmer 15 minutes longer with pot covered. When ready to serve sprinkle with chopped parsley and green onions. Serve with hot rice.

Oysters Italian

1 pint shucked oysters, drained
1/4 cup oyster water
1/2 cup Italian bread crumbs
1/2 cup grated parmesan cheese
2 cloves garlic, finely chopped
1/3 cup olive oil

Preheat oven to 325 degrees. In shallow 9 inch casserole spread 1/4 cup bread crumbs. Top with 1/4 cup Parmesan cheese, then sprinkle half of chopped garlic over the cheese. Pour half of olive oil evenly over all. Make generous layer of oysters. Add oyster water and salt if necessary. Repeat layers of bread crumbs, cheese, and garlic with olive oil. Bake for 30 minutes. Just before serving put under broiler for 5 minutes or until top is browned.

Crawfish Bouches

2 Tbsp butter
1 Tbsp minced onion
1 Tbsp minced parsley
1/4 tsp black pepper
1/2 cup bread crumbs
3/4 cup cracker meal
1 cup crawfish tails, minced
1 clove garlic, minced
1-1/2 tsp salt
1/4 tsp red pepper
1 egg, beaten
2 cups vegetable oil

Melt butter in skillet. Add onion, black pepper, garlic, salt and red pepper. Cook until vegetables are wilted. Add crawfish and cook a few minutes longer, stirring occasionally. Add bread crumbs and cracker crumbs that have soaked in the beaten egg. Test for seasoning, then add parsley. Remove from heat and let cool. Shape into small balls, and drop in 350-degree vegetable oil till golden.

Trout Amandine

2 Tbsp flour
1-1/2 tsp salt
1/4 tsp pepper
2 lbs trout or other white fish
  fillets
6 Tbsp butter
1/4 cup blanched, slivered almonds
3 Tbsp lemon juice*
1 Tbsp chopped parsley

Mix flour, 1 teaspoon salt and the pepper, sprinkle on fish. In a skillet over medium heat fry fish in 4 tablespoons butter until lightly browned, about 6 minutes. Arrange fish on warmed platter. Add remaining butter to skillet and brown almonds lightly, stirring as needed. Stir in rest of salt, lemon juice and parsley and serve at once over fish. *If desired, reduce lemon juice to 1 teaspoon and add 1/4 cup sherry.

Hush Puppies
(For Fried Seafood)

1 1/2 cup cornmeal
1/2 cup flour
2 tsp baking powder
1 tsp salt
2 eggs
1 medium onion, minced
1 clove garlic, pressed
1 (15-oz) can creamed corn
2 Tbsp olive oil

Sift the cornmeal, flour, baking powder and salt into a large bowl. Add the eggs, onion, garlic, creamed corn and olive oil. Mix well. Drop by the spoonfuls into hot vegetable oil in a deep fryer. When dark brown on one side, turn over in oil. Drain on paper towels and serve.

Poultry
&
Game

Summer Chicken

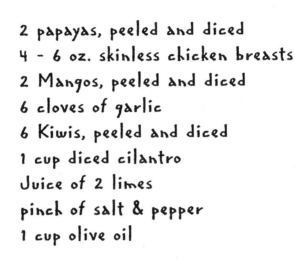

2 papayas, peeled and diced
4 - 6 oz. skinless chicken breasts
2 Mangos, peeled and diced
6 cloves of garlic
6 Kiwis, peeled and diced
1 cup diced cilantro
Juice of 2 limes
pinch of salt & pepper
1 cup olive oil

Peel the fruit and puree in processor while adding the lime juice, cilantro, garlic and seasoning till fine. Put 3/4 of the fruit mixture in a bowl and whisk the olive oil into the mixture till all is blended. Take the chicken breasts, sprinkle with salt and pepper, then brush each breast with the marinade. You can even pour some of the olive oil on top. Marinate overnight. Bake or grill chicken. This is also good sautéed, sliced and tossed with penne pasta.

Duck and Shrimp Pasta

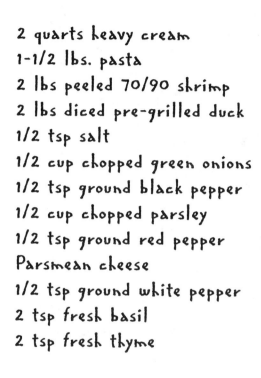

2 quarts heavy cream
1-1/2 lbs. pasta
2 lbs peeled 70/90 shrimp
2 lbs diced pre-grilled duck
1/2 tsp salt
1/2 cup chopped green onions
1/2 tsp ground black pepper
1/2 cup chopped parsley
1/2 tsp ground red pepper
Parsmean cheese
1/2 tsp ground white pepper
2 tsp fresh basil
2 tsp fresh thyme

Pour the cream into a large skillet and place over medium heat. Stir the cream when it begins to rise, keep from overflowing; when the cream comes to a boil add shrimp, duck, salt and peppers along with the fresh herbs. Heat about 8 - 10 minutes. Mixture should become very thick. Toss with pasta and top with green onions, parsley and parmesan cheese.

Chicken Creole

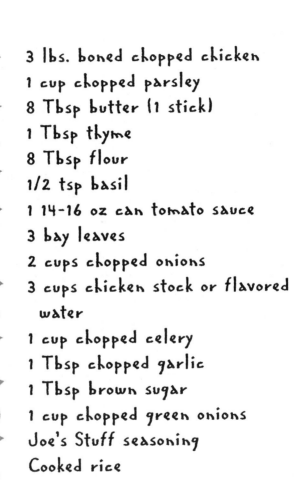

3 lbs. boned chopped chicken
1 cup chopped parsley
8 Tbsp butter (1 stick)
1 Tbsp thyme
8 Tbsp flour
1/2 tsp basil
1 14-16 oz can tomato sauce
3 bay leaves
2 cups chopped onions
3 cups chicken stock or flavored
   water
1 cup chopped celery
1 Tbsp chopped garlic
1 Tbsp brown sugar
1 cup chopped green onions
Joe's Stuff seasoning
Cooked rice

Sauté the chicken in butter for 2 - 3 minutes and remove. Add the flour and stir over medium heat until lightly browned.

Add onions, celery, green pepper and garlic and sauté vegetables until they begin to

turn transparent. Add stock, tomato sauce, thyme, basil, bay leaves, brown sugar, lemon slices and seasoning. Simmer for about 15 minutes. Add green onion, parsley and chicken during the last five minutes of cooking. Serve over rice.

Jambalaya

1/4 cup oil
1 Tbsp chopped garlic
1 cooked chicken, cut up or boned
4 cups long grain rice
1-1/2 lbs. smoked sausage
5 cups stock or flavored water
4 cups chopped onions
2 heaping tsp Joe's Stuff seasoning
2 cups chopped celery
2 cups chopped green onions or
   tomatoes (optional)
2 cups chopped green peppers

Season and brown chicken in oil (lard, bacon drippings) over medium high heat.

Add sausage to pot and sauté with chicken. Remove both from pot. For brown jambalaya, add heaping tbsp. brown sugar to hot oil and caramelize, make a roux, or use some kitchen bouquet. For red Jambalaya, add paprika for color.
Sauté onions, celery, green pepper and

garlic to the tenderness that you desire. Return chicken and sausage to pot. Add liquid and seasoning and bring to a boil.

If using kitchen bouquet for brown jambalaya, add 1 to 2 Tbsp. For red Jambalaya add approximately 1/4 cup paprika, and you may want to use 1/2 stock and 1/2 tomato juice or V-8 for your liquid. Add rice and return to boil. Cover and reduce heat to simmer. Cook for a total of 25 minutes. After 10 minutes of cooking, remove cover and quickly turn rice from top to bottom completely. Add green onions and chopped tomatoes if desired.

Note: 1 cup raw long grain rice will feed 3 people
4 Keys:
- 1 cup of rice to 1 cup of onion,1/2 cup celery and 1/2 cup green pepper;
- 1 cup raw rice to 1-1/4 cups liquid;
- Over season to compensate for the rice;
- Cook for a total 25 minutes, turning completely after 10 minutes.

If using an electric stove, reduce cooking time by 3 - 4 minutes. For seafood Jambalaya, add cooked seafood when rice is turned.

Duck a la Patout

1 Tbsp salt
3 medium onions, chopped fine
2 tsp each ground red and
   black pepper
2 medium bell peppers, chopped
1 tsp ground white pepper
1 celery rib, chopped fine
5 whole ducks, cut in half
2 cups chicken stock
2-1/2 cups all purpose flour
1 cup chopped green onions
1 cup vegetable oil
1/2 cup chopped parsley

In a small bowl, mix together the salt and peppers. Season the ducks inside and out with about half the mixture. Place the flour in a large flat pan and dredge the ducks lightly on all sides. Place the oil in a Dutch oven or other large heavy pot over medium high heat and brown the ducks well on all sides. Remove the ducks to a platter and discard all but 1 tablespoon of the oil.

Add the onions, bell peppers, and celery, reduce the heat to low, and sauté for 2 - 3 minutes. Return the ducks to the pot and add the stock. Cover the pot and let cook over lowest possible heat, or in the oven at 325 degrees until tender. Remove from heat and let stand a few minutes to allow fat to rise to the top. Skim and discard the fat. Cook remaining gravy down if necessary and keep separate from the ducks. In serving, cut out back bone and heat under broiler with gravy on top.

Duck Salad

8 - 10 Kiwis
10 duck breasts
4 Papayas
Salt and pepper
4 - 6 Mangos
2 - 3 pinches of rosemary
2 cups olive oil
1 cup chopped garlic

Peel and puree the fruit in mixer, adding a little garlic and seasoning, alternating with the fruit and blending well. Blend in the olive oil. Season the ducks with salt and pepper. Take the puree mixture and brush on duck breasts, saving 1/2 the mixture. Let marinate overnight. Grill duck skin side down to help render the fat. Slice on an angle. Serve on top of fresh mixed lettuce. Top with extra marinade.

Side Dishes

Sweet Praline Yams

1 17 oz can sweet potatoes
1 cup sugar
1/2 tsp salt
2 eggs
1/2 stick margarine
1 tsp cinnamon
1/2 cup milk
1 tsp vanilla

Topping
1 cup chopped pecans
1/3 stick margarine
1 cup brown sugar
1/3 cup flour

Preheat oven to 350 degrees.

Drain and mash potatoes, add other ingredients and place in a greased dish. Mix topping ingredients together, then pour on top of potato mixture. Bake at 350 degrees for 35 minutes.

Maque Choux

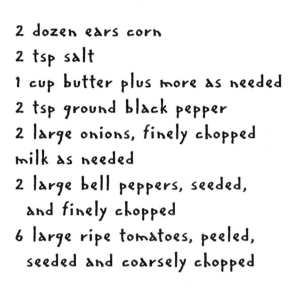

2 dozen ears corn

2 tsp salt

1 cup butter plus more as needed

2 tsp ground black pepper

2 large onions, finely chopped

milk as needed

2 large bell peppers, seeded, and finely chopped

6 large ripe tomatoes, peeled, seeded and coarsely chopped

Shuck corn. Working with one cob at a time hold it over a bowl and cut away the kernels. Then scrape the cob to release the corn milk. Melt the butter in a Dutch oven or other large heavy pot over medium high heat. Add the onions, bell peppers, and tomatoes, and sauté until the onions are translucent, about 5 minutes. Stir in the salt and pepper, then add the corn kernels and corn milk, stirring well. Reduce heat to medium and cook until the corn is tender, 20 to 30 minutes. If the mixture begins to thicken too much before corn is tender, add a little milk or butter.

Fried Tomatoes

1 egg
1/2 cup milk
2 Tomatoes, sliced
1/2 cup cornmeal
1/2 cup flour
pinch cayenne pepper
1/4 tsp salt
1/2 cup olive oil

In a bowl, mix egg and milk. In another bowl, mix the dry ingredients. Dip sliced tomatoes in egg-milk wash, then into the dry mixture. Fry in hot oil on both sides. Drain well.

Cornbread

2 eggs
1-1/2 cups milk
1-1/2 cups sifted meal
4 Tbsp flour
1 dash salt
4 Tbsp melted butter
1 tsp baking powder

Mix all the above ingredients, then pour into buttered muffin tin, or rings. Bake at 350 degrees for about 35 minutes or till a toothpick comes out clean.

Baked Tomato Casserole

8 - 10 large ripe tomatoes,
  preferably Creoles
1/4 tsp sugar
1/2 pound ground beef
2 medium bell peppers, chopped
2 medium onions, chopped
1 celery rib, chopped
2 garlic cloves, minced
salt and ground black pepper
  to taste
2 cups bread crumbs
grated Parmesan cheese

Peel and seed the tomatoes and roughly chop them. Mix in the sugar. Place a large heavy skillet over medium high heat, add the ground beef and brown well. Pour off the excess fat. Add the bell peppers, onions, celery, and garlic and sauté over medium heat until the vegetables are tender, 15 - 20 minutes. Stir in the tomatoes and simmer over low heat for about 1

hour more. Season with salt and pepper to taste, then stir in all but 1/4 cup of bread crumbs. The dressing should be fairly stiff, so add additional bread crumbs if necessary.

Pre-heat the oven to 350 degrees. Butter a medium casserole or oven proof dish. Pour in the tomato mixture and sprinkle with the remaining bread crumbs and Parmesan cheese, if desired. Place in the oven and bake until hot, about 30 minutes.

Artichoke Casserole

1/2 cup olive oil
1/2 cup onion, chopped
3 cloves garlic, chopped
1 tomato from a can of whole
   tomatoes
2 Tbsp parsley, chopped
1 cup bread crumbs
1/4 cup Parmesan cheese
1 (16 oz) can artichoke hearts
   with liquid

Sauté onion, garlic and tomato in olive oil until wilted. Add the remaining ingredients and heat. When heated, put in casserole dish and top with extra bread crumbs. Bake at 350 degrees for 15 minutes.

Carrots a la Wirth

1 pound fresh tender carrots
salt and pepper to taste
2 Tbsp butter
dash of lemon juice
1/2 cup heavy cream

Scrape and slice carrots lengthwise. Place in a saucepan and partially cover with water. Add salt, pepper, and butter. Cover and simmer until tender. Remove lid, let carrots sizzle in remaining liquid until carrots just begin to brown. Let cool slightly, add cream. Let boil and reduce until mixture thickens, just a few minutes. Add lemon juice and salt and pepper to taste.

Broccoli and Rice Casserole

1/2 cup chopped onion
1/2 cup chopped celery
1/2 cup butter
1 bag frozen chopped broccoli
2 cups uncooked rice
3/4 cup Velveeta cheese
3 cups chicken stock
1 can sliced water chestnuts, drained
1/4 cup Ritz crackers
1 bag Melts easy cheese blend

Sauté onion and celery in butter until tender, then combine in a large bowl with broccoli, rice, Velveeta, stock and water chestnuts. Top with cheese blend and bake 30-40 minutes, until bubbly and golden brown.

Desserts

Orielles de cochon
(Pig's Ears)

2 cups flour
1 tsp salt
1/2 tsp baking powder
1 Tbsp lard or butter
2/3 cup milk

Syrup
2 cups sugar
1/2 cup water
1/2 cup vinegar
1/2 cup chopped nuts

Sift dry ingredients together, then mix in the milk.

Cook all ingredients for syrup till thick.

To make orielle - roll dough out thin, and cut out squares. Drop in hot, but not smoking, oil. As mixture fries, twist and turn with a fork. As you take the orielles out, drain well, then pour 1 teaspoon of the syrup mixture over each one.

Cup Custard

5 egg yolks
3 ounces water
2 egg whites
a little salt
1 (6 oz) can evaporated milk
1 tsp vanilla
1 (6 oz) can condensed milk

Caramel
2 cups white granulated sugar

Melt sugar at low heat. Pour melted sugar into 6-8 ramekins to be used for custard.

After preparing caramel, beat egg yolks in a bowl. Stir in evaporated milk, condensed milk, water, salt and vanilla. Beat egg whites in separate bowl until firm, then add to milk and egg yolk mixture, being sure not to beat the egg whites in, just fold. Pour this mixture on top of the caramel. Place ramekins in a pan with water and bake at 350 degrees for approximately 1 -1/2 hours. Cool in refrigerator overnight. Turn upside down on plate to serve.

Meringue kisses

2 egg whites
3/4 cup sugar
1 Tbsp vanilla
6 oz. chocolate chips

Beat egg whites slightly and add sugar a little at a time until stiff. Add vanilla.

Beat, then fold in chocolate chips. Drop by small tablespoons on foil covered cookie sheet. Bake at 300 degrees 25 to 30 minutes. Makes 30 or more.

Bourbon Balls

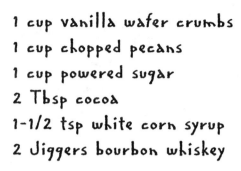

1 cup vanilla wafer crumbs
1 cup chopped pecans
1 cup powered sugar
2 Tbsp cocoa
1-1/2 tsp white corn syrup
2 Jiggers bourbon whiskey

Mix all ingredients in the order above.
Shape into bite size balls. Wrap in plastic
wrap to keep fresh.

Pralines

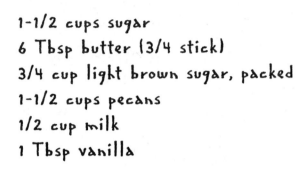

1-1/2 cups sugar
6 Tbsp butter (3/4 stick)
3/4 cup light brown sugar, packed
1-1/2 cups pecans
1/2 cup milk
1 Tbsp vanilla

Combine all ingredients in a saucepan and heat to a soft ball stage (238 - 240 degrees), stirring constantly. Remove from heat. Stir until mixture thickens and becomes creamy and cloudy, and pecans stay suspended in mixture. Spoon out on buttered waxed paper, or parchment paper. When using waxed paper, be sure to buffer with newspaper underneath, as hot wax will transfer to whatever is beneath.

Bananas Foster

4 Tbsp butter (1/2 stick)
1 cup dark brown sugar
2 bananas
2 oz. banana liqueur
4 oz. dark rum
ground cinnamon
ice cream

Melt butter in a saucepan and add brown sugar to form a creamy paste. Let this mixture caramelize over medium heat for approximately 5 minutes.

Stir in banana liqueur, bananas, and rum. Heat and ignite carefully. Agitate to keep flame burning, and add a few pinches of voodoo magic (cinnamon) to flame.

Let flame burn out, and serve over ice cream.

Pecan Pie

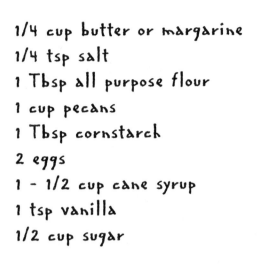

1/4 cup butter or margarine
1/4 tsp salt
1 Tbsp all purpose flour
1 cup pecans
1 Tbsp cornstarch
2 eggs
1 - 1/2 cup cane syrup
1 tsp vanilla
1/2 cup sugar

Use unbaked 9" pie shell for one pie. Melt butter, add flour and cornstarch and stir until smooth. Add syrup and sugar and boil 3 minutes. Cool. Add beaten eggs, pecans, and vanilla, blend well. Pour into pan lined with unbaked pastry. Bake in hot oven 450 degrees for 10 minutes, then reduce to 350, for 30 - 35 minutes.

Bread Pudding
With Whiskey Sauce

1 10 oz. loaf stale French bread, crumbled

2 tsp vanilla

1 cup raisins

4 cups milk

1 cup coconut

2 cups sugar

1 cup chopped pecans

8 Tbsp butter, melted

1 tsp cinnamon

3 eggs

1 tsp nutmeg

Combine all ingredients. Mixture should be very moist but not soupy. Pour into buttered 9" x 12" baking dish or larger. Place into non-preheated oven. Bake at 350 degrees for approximately 1 hour and 15 minutes, until top is golden brown. Serve warm with whiskey sauce.

Whiskey Sauce

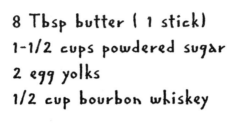

8 Tbsp butter (1 stick)
1-1/2 cups powdered sugar
2 egg yolks
1/2 cup bourbon whiskey

Cream butter and sugar over medium heat until all butter is absorbed. Remove from heat and blend in egg yolk. Pour in bourbon gradually to your own taste, stirring constantly. Sauce will thicken as it cools.

For a variety of sauces, just substitute your favorite fruit juice or liqueur for the bourbon.

Heavenly Hash

1 large package of Hershey's semi sweet tidbits (12 oz.)
1 large package of miniature marshmallows
1 (6 oz) can condensed milk
2 cups of broken pecans

Melt the chocolate tidbits over low heat. When melted, remove from heat and add condensed milk, mixing well. Add pecans, then fold in marshmallows and pour into buttered 9-inch square dish. Refrigerate.

Devil's Food Cake

5 eggs
1 cup of butter
2-1/2 cups sugar
3 cups of flour
1 tsp baking powder
1 cup buttermilk
pinch of baking soda
1 cup powdered cocoa
1 tsp salt

In mixer, cream butter and sugar, while adding 1 egg at a time. Sift flour and baking powder with soda and salt. Add to cake batter, alternating with buttermilk. Fold in chocolate. Pour into 9-inch round cake pans. Bake at 350 degrees for 25 minutes. Makes three layers.

Icing:

8 ounces baker's chocolate
3 cups sugar
1 cup milk
1/2 stick butter
2 Tbsp white caro syrup

Cook above ingredients till they form a soft ball. Cool thoroughly before using.

Pecans with this icing are delicious.

Beignets, Michael's Way

Pinch Salt
2 cups flour
2 Tbsp baking powder
2 Tbsp sugar
2 Tbsp butter melted
2 lg. eggs separated
4 lg. McIntosh or Granny Smith
  Apples
1-1/2 cans beer (cold)

Peel, core and slice (1/4" thick) apples. Mix all dry ingredients. Add egg yolks and butter to dry mixture. Add beer slowly and mix until thick batter is created (may not need all the beer). Whip egg whites till stiff. Soften batter with a little of the egg whites. Gently fold in eggwhites. Coat apple rings with batter and deep fry in clean oil. Sprinkle with powdered sugar. Serve hot. Drink the remaining beer. (It's only 6 ounces!)

Café Brulot

Peel of 1 orange, broken into
  10 or 12 pieces
10 cloves
4 sticks of cinnamon, 4 inches
  long, broken in pieces
3/4 cup plus 1 Tbsp cognac
14 lumps of sugar
2 cups hot strong black coffee

Place first 5 ingredients into the Cafe
Brulot bowl. Fill a metal tablespoon with
cognac. Hold lighted match underneath
spoon and ignite contents of bowl with
burning cognac. Ladle high for effect. Stir
and ladle high over the bowl. Pour coffee
into 10 demitasse cups. Serve immediately.

Cocktails

Scarlett O'Hara

1 jigger (1-1/2 oz) Southern
   Comfort
juice of 1/2 fresh lime
1/2 jigger (3/4 oz.) Ocean Spray
   cranberry juice

Shake well with cracked ice.
Strain into cocktail glass.

Mint Julep

6 sprigs fresh mint
1 tsp syrup

Crush mint leaves gently with a spoon;
add

1 jigger of rye whiskey

Shake and strain into glass with a sprig of
mint.

Alexander

1 Tbsp 1/2 oz fresh cream
3/4 oz. cream de cacao
1 jigger whiskey, gin or brandy

Shake ingredients well with cracked ice
and strain into cocktail glass

Southern Egg Nog

3 cups sugar
12 egg yolks
1 qt. whiskey
1 qt. heavy cream
dash nutmeg

Mix 3 cups of sugar with yolks of 12 eggs.
Drip a quart of Kentucky whiskey into the
mixture, stirring slowly and constantly.
Whip one quart of heavy cream stiff and
stir into whiskey mixture. Pour into glasses
and sprinkle with nutmeg.

Appetizers

Soups & Gumbos

Brunch

Seafood

Poultry & Game

Side Dishes

Desserts

Cocktails

★ New Orleans School of Cooking
    Signature Dishes